POISONS IN OUR PATH

Anne Ophelia Dowden

POISONS IN OUR PATH

PLANTS THAT HARM AND HEAL

HarperCollins*Publishers*

ACKNOWLEDGMENTS

Most of the illustrations in this book are based on my research paintings made over many years and in many places, and I want to thank again all the people who helped me obtain those living specimens. In collecting a number of new plants, I have received valuable help from Dr. Stephen K-M Tim at the Brooklyn Botanic Garden, from Mr. Panayoti Kelaidis and Dr. William Gambill at the Denver Botanic Gardens, and from Mr. John Moore, Mr. and Mrs. William Royal, and Mrs. Helen Phillips in Colorado fields and gardens. For technical information and advice I am greatly indebted to University of Colorado faculty members Dr. William Weber, Professor Emeritus of Natural History, and Dr. Glenn Appelt, Professor of Pharmacy. And very special thanks are due Dr. Peter Nelson, Professor Emeritus of Botany, Brooklyn College, for his advice, encouragement, and careful reading of my manuscript.

All plants pictured are exactly ½ natural size.

Library of Congress Cataloging-in-Publication Data
Dowden, Anne Ophelia Todd, date
  Poisons in our path : plants that harm and heal / Anne Ophelia Dowden.
    p.   cm.
  Summary: Describes the physical characteristics and natural habitats of several varieties of plants, as well as their poisonous, medical, and magical properties.
  ISBN 0-06-020861-9. — ISBN 0-06-020862-7 (lib. bdg.)
  1. Poisonous plants—Juvenile literature. 2. Medicinal plants—Juvenile literature. 3. Poisonous plants—Folklore—Juvenile literature. 4. Medicinal plants—Folklore—Juvenile literature. [1. Poisonous plants. 2. Medicinal plants.] I. Title.
QK100.A1D68 1994   92-9518
581.6'9—dc20   CIP
                                  AC

1 2 3 4 5 6 7 8 9 10
❖
First Edition

CONTENTS

SNOW-ON-THE-MOUNTAIN
Euphorbia marginata

All members of the euphorbia, or spurge, family have a milky sap that can cause bad skin eruptions. Many wild euphorbias are small and dull, but others, like poinsettia and crown of thorns, are beautiful houseplants. Snow-on-the-mountain, a western wild plant, is now grown in gardens all over the United States.

POINSETTIA
Euphorbia pulcherrima

6

CROWN OF THORNS
Euphorbia splendens

DEADLY HARVEST

It is hard to believe that the gentle green world around us is not entirely friendly. We do not expect to find dangers there. Even so, our earliest human ancestors, about a half million years ago, approached it cautiously. They were well aware of the fierce and bloody threats of the animal world, where they fought for safety as well as for food, and at first even the green kingdom was intimidating.

But as those hunters stalked their game, they found berries and nuts and roots, sampled them, and discovered that such things were good to eat too. Ages passed while they tried out various plants, noted successes and failures, and gradually learned what they could eat or smoke, smear on arrows, or rub on a wound.

From those earliest beginnings to the present day, human beings have owed their entire existence to the green world. Plants provide most of the oxygen we breathe, much of our clothing and shelter, and all of our food (since the animals we eat, eat plants in their turn). Plants have given us nearly everything we use in our daily lives, from medicines to dyes, pens to paper, building materials to perfumes.

And plants gave us poisons—poisons that can make people sick or unconscious or delirious, can burn or irritate the skin, even kill. Our ancestors discovered that such substances were dangerous and frightening, but also useful. Managed carefully, they freed houses from vermin, killed enemies, and provided nearly all medicines. And, of course, they became the important tools of witches and of priests and sorcerers who combated evil spirits.

These toxic plants played their part in history from the time of the Assyrians and Egyptians onward. In medieval and Renaissance Europe all herbalists wrote about them. Greek doctors used them, and so do the doctors of today. The ancient poisonous plants known in European lore and legend have nearly all traveled to America. Here they grow chiefly in our gardens, though some have escaped and can now be found wild in our woods and fields. But the Americas—North and South—also contributed their own toxic harvest. Our gardens and our countrysides are full of these dangerous plants, and making their acquaintance is important. Many can harm us, many are useful, and all of them are interesting.

But in making that acquaintance, it is extremely important to identify the plants correctly. Their common names are not reliable. A single plant species can have a dozen different labels in as many different places, and sometimes the same common name is used for several different plants. Only its scientific binomial identifies a plant exactly, and when we are dealing with poisons, exactness is important.

PHILODENDRON
Philodendron oxycardium

THE POISONS

A surprisingly large number of the world's plants contain the toxic substances that can kill any creature that eats enough of them. Most of these plants never affect human beings because very few of us go around tasting the leaves we find in pastures and woodlands—certainly not eating quantities sufficient to harm us. But some poisonous plants with attractive berries or succulent roots do tempt nibblers. And some can damage us in other ways.

No one is entirely sure why plants have these poisons, which play no part in the growing and fruiting process. The toxins are an incidental by-product of that process, but they have become a protection against animals and people. Some plants even poison the soil and thus kill all nearby growth that could smother them or compete for nutrients.

Of the plants that threaten people, one group acts only by contact. Their poisonous substances are crystals or chemicals

9

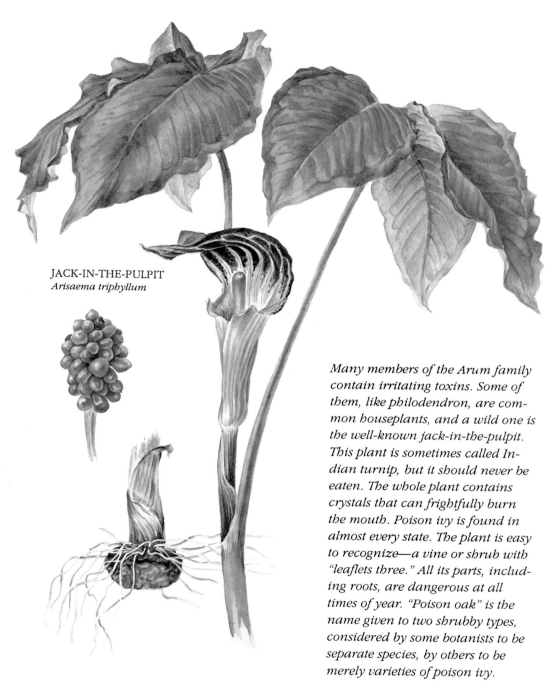

JACK-IN-THE-PULPIT
Arisaema triphyllum

Many members of the Arum family contain irritating toxins. Some of them, like philodendron, are common houseplants, and a wild one is the well-known jack-in-the-pulpit. This plant is sometimes called Indian turnip, but it should never be eaten. The whole plant contains crystals that can frightfully burn the mouth. Poison ivy is found in almost every state. The plant is easy to recognize—a vine or shrub with "leaflets three." All its parts, including roots, are dangerous at all times of year. "Poison oak" is the name given to two shrubby types, considered by some botanists to be separate species, by others to be merely varieties of poison ivy.

10

so irritating that they can produce severe sores and rashes on the skin of many people. They are generally not deadly, but if eaten, they can kill by making the throat swell to the point of suffocation. Many members of the Euphorbia family, such as poinsettia and crown of thorns, have this kind of toxin in their sap, and so do many members of the Arum family, including jack-in-the-pulpit, philodendron, and dumbcane.

Poison ivy and poison oak cause even more serious rashes, and they are usually included among toxic plants even though they are not truly poisonous. Such rashes are caused

POISON IVY
Toxicodendron radicans

by an allergic reaction to nonpoisonous oils in leaves and stems, in the same way that hay fever is an allergic reaction to the pollen in flowers. Not everyone is sensitive to them, and even a sensitive person's reaction can vary from time to time. But these plants are extremely common, and their effects can be very bad indeed; so it is important to recognize them and stay away from any kind of contact with them. Even indirect contact can be dangerous: The irritating oils can be carried on clothing or borne in smoke when the plants are burned. Poison sumac is a close relative of poison ivy and is even more dangerous, but it grows only in very wet swamps where few people are likely to meet it.

However, these are not the deadly plant poisons. The ones that can kill us are those that damage internal tissues or interfere with the way the body works. When swallowed, some affect the blood or the muscles or the nervous system. Some, like castor bean, affect the digestive system and produce vomiting and diarrhea. Foxglove stimulates the heart; lily of the valley causes it to beat irregularly. Some of the most deadly ones attack the central nervous system and can cause delirium, convulsions, or paralysis. Many affect several parts of the body: False hellebore works on the higher nerve centers and thus slows the heartbeat. It can also damage the digestive system, and it is intensely narcotic. Of course, the dangerous power that such plants exercise over bodily functions is the very quality that makes many of them useful medicines. For instance, castor oil's powerful effect on the intestines has

CASTOR BEAN
Ricinus communis

Castor oil comes from the seeds of the castor bean. This handsome plant originated in tropical Africa and succeeds best in warm climates, but it can be grown in northern gardens. Castor seeds have been found in Egyptian tombs, and since ancient times, the oil has been used medicinally, chiefly as a purgative. Today, it is much more important in the manufacture of many commercial products and as a lubricant. Eating three of its seeds can kill a man.

13

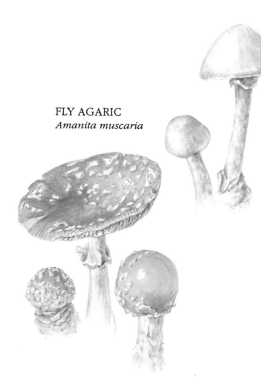

DEADLY AMANITA
Amanita virosa

FLY AGARIC
Amanita muscaria

Many mushrooms are quite harmless, but identifying them is often difficult. Even specialists disagree on some species of Amanita, the group that causes the greatest number of deaths. Deadly amanita, or destroying angel, brings delirium, convulsions, and usually death. Fly agaric was at one time used as a medicine for respiratory ailments. But it produces raving drunkenness and hallucinations, and in northern Europe it was popular as a means of intoxication.

made it, for centuries, one of the commonest remedies for constipation.

Poisons of the various mushrooms attack various parts of the body, especially the nervous, respiratory, and circulatory systems. Of all plant groups, mushrooms are possibly the most dangerous because people like to gather them for gourmet meals. But so many are toxic, and their poisons are so deadly, that no one should ever sample any wild mushroom unless it has been identified by an expert botanist. It is not true, as many people believe, that a silver spoon, placed in a pan of cooking mushrooms, will turn dark if the mushrooms are poisonous.

14

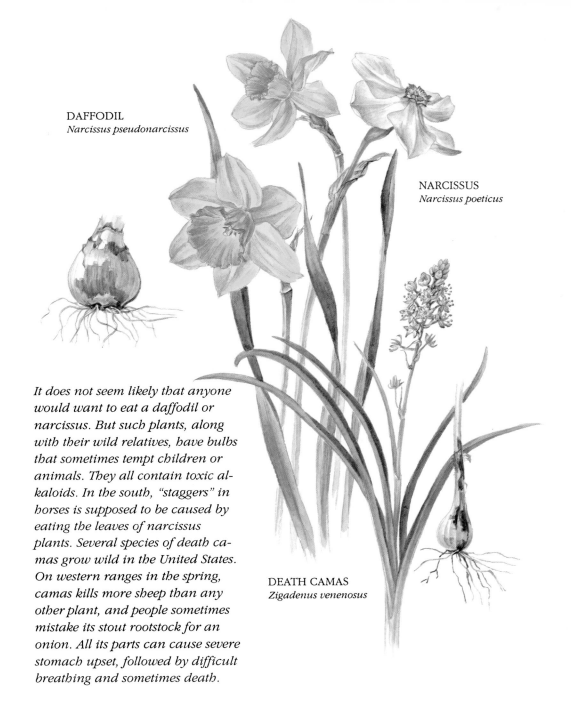

DAFFODIL
Narcissus pseudonarcissus

NARCISSUS
Narcissus poeticus

DEATH CAMAS
Zigadenus venenosus

It does not seem likely that anyone would want to eat a daffodil or narcissus. But such plants, along with their wild relatives, have bulbs that sometimes tempt children or animals. They all contain toxic alkaloids. In the south, "staggers" in horses is supposed to be caused by eating the leaves of narcissus plants. Several species of death camas grow wild in the United States. On western ranges in the spring, camas kills more sheep than any other plant, and people sometimes mistake its stout rootstock for an onion. All its parts can cause severe stomach upset, followed by difficult breathing and sometimes death.

15

WILD BLACK CHERRY
Prunus serotina

The wild black cherry is a very common tree in the eastern United States. Its black fruits are edible and they are often used for wine or jelly, but their seeds are dangerous. Also toxic are the cherry's wilting leaves and small white flowers. Their cyanide-producing amygdalin has an odor like bitter almonds.

Of course, to be damaged by any of these internal poisons, one must eat the plants—often eat a lot of them—and usually only certain parts. In daffodil and death camas, the roots, or bulbs, are especially poisonous. Very commonly, a plant's leaves and bark contain the toxin, as in oleander and thorn apple. Sometimes it is in the seeds, as in castor bean and horse chestnut. Only occasionally is a plant uniformly poisonous.

Sometimes harmless substances in a plant become toxic under certain conditions. The seeds, leaves, and bark of cherries

16

and related fruits such as apples, peaches, and pears, all contain amygdalin. Harmless in itself, in the digestive system it breaks down into several compounds. One of these is cyanide or prussic acid—a favorite poison in many murder stories.

Often, poison is present only in certain stages of a plant's growth. The very young shoots of milkweed and pokeweed, and the fiddleheads of some ferns, cooked like asparagus, are spring delicacies for many country gourmets; but when mature, these plants are all dangerous. Some western milkweeds, in fact, are among our most deadly plants.

Milkweed poison is a boon to monarch butterflies. Their young caterpillars, hatched from eggs laid on milkweed leaves, eat only those leaves. Unaffected by the toxin, they store it in their bodies, and when they become butterflies, they are so poisonous that birds never eat them.

Larkspur leaves are very poisonous when young, but scarcely so at all when they are older. Alder trees are known to produce toxins only when they are attacked by insects. And some plants are dangerous only when they grow in certain soils. They can absorb from the earth poisonous minerals, such as selenium and copper, and concentrate them a thousandfold in their leaves.

Plants with powers like these have, of course, been very important to human beings. There are hundreds of them in the United States—thousands around the world—and over the years they have played their part in the big events of history

MILKWEED
Asclepias syriaca

All milkweeds have leaves that are poisonous to eat. Animals generally do not like the milky juice that contains the poison, and they avoid the plants except when other green things are not available. But a handful of leaves can kill a sheep. Even so, this common eastern milkweed is a popular spring vegetable when its young shoots are just appearing above the ground. They should always be well cooked. Several western milkweeds are effective heart stimulants, and some are still used in Hispanic folk medicine.

POKEWEED
Phytolacca americana

The young shoots of pokeweed have for centuries been gathered in the spring and eaten like asparagus. If carefully cooked, they make a safe and pleasant potherb. But the very large root is extremely poisonous, and the mature leaves and berries can produce convulsions and death. The plant has been used in medicine as a powerful narcotic, emetic, and purgative, and recently it has proved promising as a treatment for AIDS. In Portugal at one time, wine was colored with the deep-purple juice of the berries.

and the small routines of daily living. For centuries, red squill was used as a rat poison, and today pyrethrum flowers furnish an excellent plant spray that kills insect pests but does not harm warm-blooded animals, including people.

In Europe, monkshood was called wolfsbane because country people used it to poison wolves. It was also a part of the equipment of Renaissance noblemen and all others who might want to do away with themselves or their enemies, or hasten an inheritance. From the time of Augustus Caesar to the Borgias, monkshood's active ingredient, aconitine, was considered the deadliest of all poisons. Romeo drank aconite

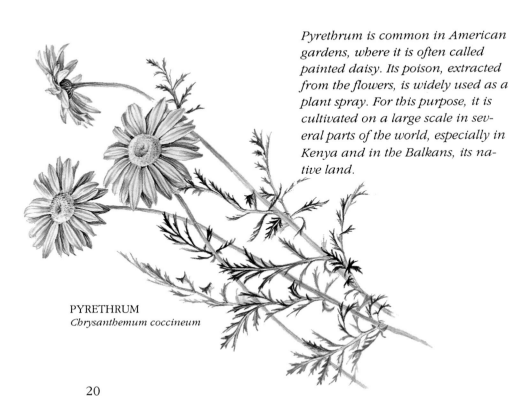

Pyrethrum is common in American gardens, where it is often called painted daisy. Its poison, extracted from the flowers, is widely used as a plant spray. For this purpose, it is cultivated on a large scale in several parts of the world, especially in Kenya and in the Balkans, its native land.

PYRETHRUM
Chrysanthemum coccineum

in despair when he thought that Juliet was dead. And on the Greek island Khíos, old men were made to swallow it when they became infirm and no longer useful to the state. Until recently, aconite was an important drug in official medicine.

Other beautiful garden plants share this lurid past. Azaleas and rhododendrons contain a deadly poison. Primitive people pounded azalea leaves into a pulp and threw it into ponds to paralyze fish and make them easier to catch, and the azalea also played a part in the course of European history. In 401 B.C. the brilliant general Xenophon led ten thousand Greek soldiers on a campaign through Asia Minor and wrote a famous account of it. Two days' march in from the seacoast, his army camped in a village with many beehives, and the tired and hungry men ate lots of honey, which was made from the nectar of Pontic azaleas. Soon some "were like men drunk," others "were like madmen and some like dying persons." Fortunately for Xenophon, his men recovered in a few days, before any enemy attacked.

But 300 years later, the Roman general Pompey was not so lucky. Pompey's campaign against Rome's ancient enemy, the kingdom of Pontus, progressed well until his armies camped near Trebizond, almost exactly where Xenophon's weary soldiers had stopped to forage. The Roman soldiers also ate the poisoned honey, and in their disabled state they were set upon and massacred by the Pontic army. So the power of the mighty Roman Empire was halted for a time by a lovely but dangerous shrub.

MONKSHOOD
Aconitum napellus

*Legend says that monkshood sprang
from the frothing saliva of Cerberus,
the dog that guards the gates of
Hades. From every part of the plant
come alkaloids that powerfully de-
press the heart and were until recently an official drug. In ancient
times, monkshood was used by
armies to poison wells. In India it
was an arrow poison for lion
hunters and in Europe a wolf and
rat bait. The ancient European
monkshood now grows commonly
in North American gardens, but
there are several very poisonous
wild species of* Aconitum *in the
western United States.*

22

Honey made from this azalea was so "venomous and deadly" that the Pontic people never sold it, though they regularly exported large amounts of bee's wax to the Romans. All over the world, various species of azalea and rhododendron were for centuries the curse of herdsmen. Cattle, sheep, and goats died from eating the leaves. From Italy to Japan, those leaves were used to treat various ailments, from asthma to rheumatism. Finally, modern research discovered that, given in tiny doses, they were effective in lowering blood pressure.

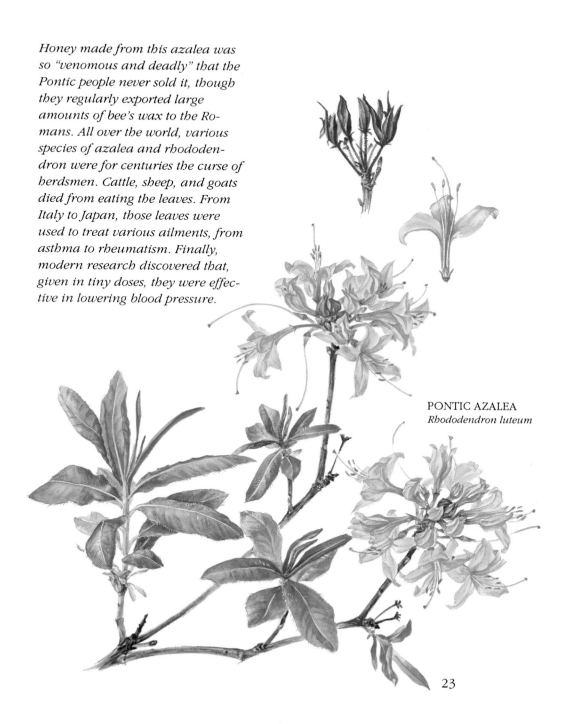

PONTIC AZALEA
Rhododendron luteum

23

Another deadly toxin comes from poison hemlock, an ancient plant that now grows all over the world. Every part of it contains the poisonous alkaloid coniine, which until recent times was used in medicine as a sedative and antispasmodic. Ancient Greeks who wanted to commit suicide crowned themselves with laurel and drank a cup of hemlock, and it was also used to dispatch criminals. Hemlock was the poisonous drink executioners gave to the Greek philosopher and teacher, Socrates, when he was condemned to death for corrupting the minds of the young.

For centuries, plants like these were part of the folklore, science, and commerce of Europe and Asia. Then, with the exploration of the New World, a new world of plants was also discovered. In Central and South America, botanists and doctors accompanied the conquering Spanish armies to collect and take home with them hundreds of plants they found the Indians using. Along with corn, rubber, and potatoes, they found the arrow poison curare, the narcotic coca (source of cocaine), and many others.

In North America, the English came as settlers rather than conquerors. They brought their own plants, but they too learned from the Indians. They discovered that Indians ate the poisonous jack-in-the-pulpit roots, but only after boiling or baking the corms, cutting them into fine pieces, drying them, then rebaking them, thus destroying the toxin. These settlers in New England found that the leaves of mountain laurel have a poison similar to that of its relatives, azalea and

Poison hemlock is a tall, beautiful member of the carrot family, quite unrelated to the American tree called hemlock. Its virulent poison kills by gradually paralyzing the motor nerves, leaving the mind unaffected to the end. Hemlock was a devil's plant and a favorite of all witches. Pliny says that serpents avoid it, and the herbalist John Gerard calls it "evill, dangerous, hurtfull." Children have been poisoned by whistles and blowpipes made from its hollow, purple-splotched stems.

POISON HEMLOCK
Conium maculatum

25

rhododendron. One species of laurel was used by the Indians for suicide, and another is still called lambkill because it is so dangerous to animals.

The colonists also learned that some other beautiful wild plants should not be eaten. Most irises, both wild and cultivated, contain in their leaves and underground stems a very irritating substance that causes severe digestive upsets. Buttercups have a similar irritant. Larkspur seeds were once used medicinally in Europe, but the many wild larkspur species in North America are among our most poisonous plants, especially in the west.

MOUNTAIN LAUREL
Kalmia latifolia

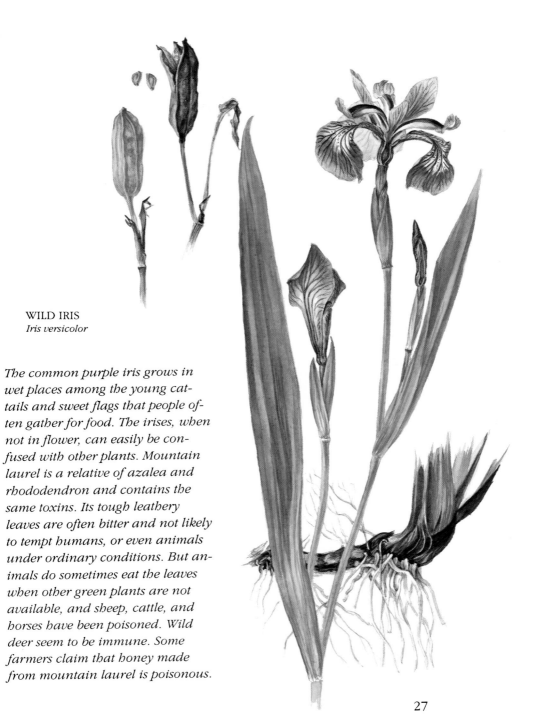

WILD IRIS
Iris versicolor

The common purple iris grows in wet places among the young cattails and sweet flags that people often gather for food. The irises, when not in flower, can easily be confused with other plants. Mountain laurel is a relative of azalea and rhododendron and contains the same toxins. Its tough leathery leaves are often bitter and not likely to tempt humans, or even animals under ordinary conditions. But animals do sometimes eat the leaves when other green plants are not available, and sheep, cattle, and horses have been poisoned. Wild deer seem to be immune. Some farmers claim that honey made from mountain laurel is poisonous.

27

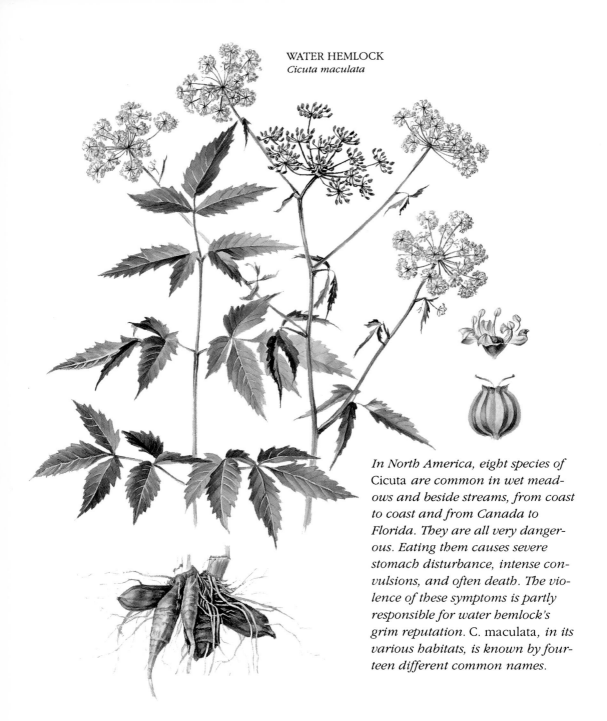

WATER HEMLOCK
Cicuta maculata

In North America, eight species of Cicuta *are common in wet meadows and beside streams, from coast to coast and from Canada to Florida. They are all very dangerous. Eating them causes severe stomach disturbance, intense convulsions, and often death. The violence of these symptoms is partly responsible for water hemlock's grim reputation.* C. maculata, *in its various habitats, is known by fourteen different common names.*

28

And the early settlers encountered water hemlock, possibly the most virulent poisonous plant in North America. Its toxin is found in all its parts, but especially in the roots. They grow in clumps, like dahlia roots, and they smell like parsnips. In winter, when they are swollen and succulent, people sometimes mistake them for wild parsnips. But one mouthful can kill a man. Though these roots are easily recognized, the plant as a whole is very hard to distinguish from its many relatives in the carrot family, some of which have almost identical flowers.

Discoveries like these were valuable to the eastern colonists, but those settlers had so many of their own traditional plants that they were not seriously affected by the wild things growing around them. Their problems were small compared to the enormous difficulties American pioneers encountered later as they moved westward and opened up new lands for pasture. In the central states, and then on western prairies, they met hundreds of plants they did not know. Sometimes entire herds of cattle died after eating larkspur. Sheep were killed by halogeton. Sheep, cows, and goats ate St. John's-wort and were so damaged by its photosensitizing chemicals that they suffered terrible burns from sunlight.

Horses went crazy from locoweed. From the earliest pioneering days, ranchers were puzzled when cattle, sheep, and especially horses became erratic and violent, and thousands died. Finally scientific research located the poison in a group of plants in the pea family. More than six hundred different

ST. JOHN'S-WORT
Hypericum perforatum

LOCOWEED
Oxytropis lambertii

In ancient Europe, St. John's-wort was not only a charm against evil but also a universal balm—a cure for all ills. Animals there, not subjected to intense sun, were not harmed by it. "Loco" is a Spanish word meaning "crazy," and it describes the effect of locoweed on horses, cattle, and sheep. Locoweed disease has been known ever since people began to colonize the Great Plains of the United States, and it is still a problem.

species of these plants grow in North America, and only a botanist can identify them all and tell which ones are poisonous. The damage from the locos was so great that the state of Colorado once placed a bounty on their roots. Ranchers soon found that this was a potential gold mine. They could pull up a plant with part of its root, turn it in and collect their money. Next spring a new plant was growing from the part left in the ground—another bounty. Threatened with bankruptcy, the state rescinded its offer.

All these dangerous plants were a problem chiefly for ranchers and farmers, and in general, poisonous plants have always threatened animals more than they threaten people. People do not often eat enough wild leaves or roots to suffer serious consequences.

But a few plants do threaten us. For instance, in the south, men cutting down manchineel trees have been blinded by the sap. Ergot, a very poisonous fungus that grows in the heads of wheat, rye, and other grains, can be harvested along with the grain and made into flour. And sometimes the poison reaches us indirectly: When states like Illinois, Indiana, and Ohio were frontiers and their forests were being cut and replaced by pastures, a malady called milk sickness reached epidemic proportions in farm communities. Thousands of people were sick and many died, among them Abraham Lincoln's mother, Nancy Hanks. Some communities lost half their members. Cattle died or got the "trembles," and no one knew the cause of the mysterious illness. Not until the 1900s did

ROSARY PEA
Abrus precatorius

Rosary pea, or precatory pea, is a widespread vine in the tropics. It is now grown in Florida for its handsome, but very poisonous, seeds. In India, the seeds were used as jeweler's weights, and often they were ground into powder and smeared on daggers.

houseplants, dumbcane can irritate or paralyze the throat with its sharp crystals, and hyacinth bulbs can fatally attack the digestive system. In the garden, daphne berries, the foliage of box, and sweet-pea pods can kill a child. Even the vegetable garden has its dangers. The green leaf blades of rhubarb are very poisonous, though the red stems are safe and delicious. Tomato and potato belong to the deadly nightshade family and contain some of that family's toxic solanine. The amounts are so small as to be negligible, except occasionally in the skins of potato tubers (the part we eat). If potatoes are allowed to become green—usually when stored in light places—they can be seriously toxic. And seeds of apples and most of their relatives—cherries, peaches, apricots—produce deadly cyanide.

34

But none of these plants, however virulent their poison, will do us the slightest harm if we know them and respect them. We must simply understand that it is very important *never* to eat any plant, wild or tame, that we do not positively know to be safe. But after all, eating is not part of the everyday enjoyment of wayside plants. The poison stored in some beautiful growing things has nothing whatever to do with our normal pleasure in the green life we meet in all our fields and woods and gardens.

Ornamental daphnes were introduced from Europe into American gardens, but they often escape into woods and thickets. Their bark, leaves, and fruits contain a toxic glucoside, and children have died from eating the pretty red berries. The bark has been used in medicine. The plant is named for the nymph Daphne, who changed into a laurel tree to escape Apollo's lovemaking.

DAPHNE
Daphne giraldii

YEW
Taxus cuspidata

Yew was both loved and feared. Its wood was valued for spear shafts and bows, and it was planted near houses and churches to protect them against magic. But it was also a tree of evil, associated with funerals. All its parts can poison animals, but the seed in the bright red "berry" is the most toxic.

THE MAGIC

When those first primitive human beings, so long ago, began to look with curiosity at the green world around them, they approached it timidly, with the same awe they felt for all the forces of nature. They did not understand those forces and viewed them with fear, believing that the supernatural beings inhabiting them were mostly sinister, or at least mischievous. This hostile world terrified men and women. They felt powerless to face it alone and so turned hopefully to magic. Throughout history and around the world, magic influenced people's lives and shaped the folklore of every land.

In the beginning, nearly all plants were gathered with a prayer, and some were gathered only by priests and sorcerers. These men were often the most intelligent and observant members of a community, and they were the first to discover the properties of plants. They became the first doctors, and many of their herbal remedies have remained as recognized drugs to the present day. But of course they also used many "remedies" that were pure fancy, part of the web of magic that was expected to keep the powers of darkness from interfering with people's daily lives—all their activities from household to cowshed. Almost every plant that grows had some supposed power, but the most valued ones were often the poisons.

Priests and magicians were inclined to keep their knowledge of poisons and medicines a closely guarded secret to use for their own mysterious ends. Most of all they valued the plants that could produce delirium and what appeared to be supernatural ecstasies. The trances and prophetic ravings of the oracle and priests of Apollo at Delphi, for instance, were chiefly caused by thorn apple. Thus the most sacred and treasured plants were usually the ones we still know to be seriously toxic. They were regarded as the special property of the Devil and of the three most powerful witches of legend—Hecate, Circe, and Medea.

Hecate, Greek goddess of the underworld, represented the darkness and terrors of the night. She was queen of sorcery and witchcraft, feared throughout Europe for centuries. She appears in Shakespeare's play *Macbeth* when, under her direction, three witches meet Macbeth on a lonely Scottish heath. While a powerful brew boils in their cauldron, they call up apparitions to foretell his bloody fate. Their brew is a complicated one, with twenty-three ingredients, from eye of newt to wool of bat to nose of Turk. It contains two herbs—slips of yew and "root of hemlock, digg'd i' the dark."

Homer tells us how Circe turned the wandering Ulysses' men into pigs. When the sailors landed on her island, she entertained them with a feast and a potion containing "pernicious drugs." Ulysses himself was able to rescue them only because the god Hermes had given him a magic herb that protected him from Circe's spell.

Medea, daughter of the king of Colchis, befriended the hero Jason when he came in search of the Golden Fleece. She gave him a spell to help him slay the fire-breathing bulls that guarded it, and after he succeeded in his task, she eloped with him. One of her favorite herbs was colchicum, or autumn crocus, but she also used monkshood, alkanet, juniper, and many others.

Powerful witches like these could force even the gods to yield to their demands, and mere humans were quite helpless against their spells. But there were also innumerable lesser witches believed to be lurking in every countryside, and these evil creatures could interfere with every aspect of human life. They invaded households, turned milk sour, kidnapped babies, caused illnesses or accidents. So it was important for everyone to know what herbs to use to "hinder witches from their will," to enable a person to see witches and fairies, or even to make himself invisible. The charms were applied in many different ways: sometimes brewed into drinks, but very often hung in the house or worn around the neck.

Collars of climbing nightshade were placed around the necks of horses, cows, and pigs, and the herbalist Nicholas

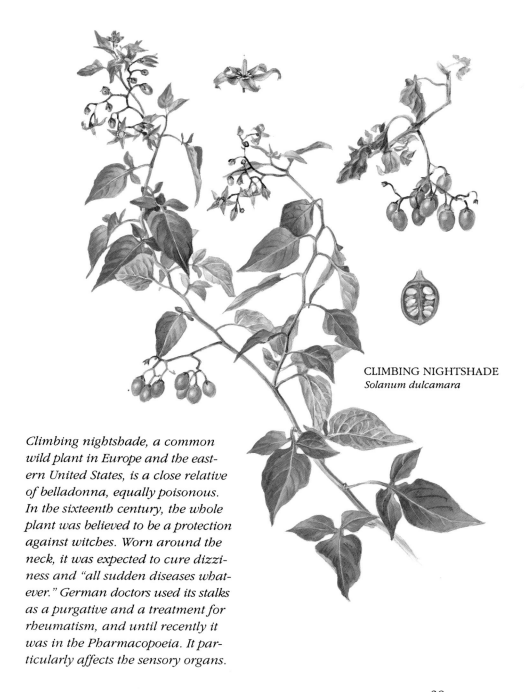

CLIMBING NIGHTSHADE
Solanum dulcamara

Climbing nightshade, a common wild plant in Europe and the eastern United States, is a close relative of belladonna, equally poisonous. In the sixteenth century, the whole plant was believed to be a protection against witches. Worn around the neck, it was expected to cure dizziness and "all sudden diseases whatever." German doctors used its stalks as a purgative and a treatment for rheumatism, and until recently it was in the Pharmacopoeia. It particularly affects the sensory organs.

39

Culpepper wrote that this nightshade was "excellent good to remove witchcrafts both in man and beasts." English ivy was considered a plant of good omen, which kept evil away from milk, butter, and farm animals. In Germany, it always decked the necks of cattle when they were first driven out to pasture in the spring.

Mistletoe is such a strange plant, growing as a parasite on trees and remaining green all winter, that it was inevitably

All parts of the ivy plant are toxic. Children have been poisoned by the berries, and clippings from the vines have made animals sick. In Greece, ivy was sacred to Bacchus, who wore it in a crown, as an antidote to drunkenness. Always a beneficent plant, ivy was a symbol of love and friendship. In France, it was one of the herbs of St. John, gathered before the festive fires were lit on Midsummer Eve. And, with holly, ivy was used to deck houses and churches at Christmastime.

ENGLISH IVY
Hedera helix

40

endowed with magic powers. It kept witches away and bestowed innumerable benefits, from promoting fertility and calming epileptic fits to opening locks and improving the apple harvest. Mistletoe was revered by the Romans, and the Druids gathered it with the greatest reverence when they found it growing on their sacred oak trees. Finally, early Christians adopted it and made it a symbol of the Christmas season, though not of Christmas Day itself.

European mistletoe has been revered since Roman times, and it has always been considered a supremely magical plant. The Druids cut it from oak trees with a golden sickle, catching it in a white cloak so that it did not touch the ground. Though poisonous, it was widely used in treating convulsions and other nervous disorders. American mistletoe never accumulated such legends, but it has the same toxins and the same uses. Its berries have brought death to children who ate them.

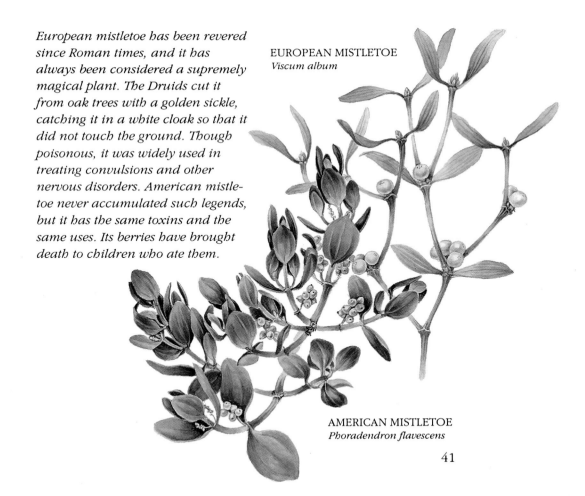

EUROPEAN MISTLETOE
Viscum album

AMERICAN MISTLETOE
Phoradendron flavescens

41

Elaborate rules governed the collecting and use of all these magic plants. They were often gathered in graveyards, nearly always at specific seasons of the year or phases of the moon, at certain times of the day or in places where the sun never shone. Mixed into potions, they were combined in prescribed numbers, often seven or nine.

But not all magic makers were baleful black witches. White magic was often practiced by the village herbwomen. They were well acquainted with wild plants and garden herbs and all the home remedies such herbs provided, and they regularly treated their sick neighbors. But they often received their greatest income from the sale of love potions and spells to reveal the future. They knew what plants a maiden should put under her pillow to bring dreams of her future husband, and also how to brew a potion that would entrap a reluctant lover. Love philters, of course, did not include poisonous plants, but white magic had many uses even for the toxic herbs. Christmas rose, for instance, drove away the evil spirits that could damage people and their possessions—sicken their cattle or wither their harvest. Tansy leaves worn in the shoe prevented chills and fever. A sprig of mugwort in the pocket prevented weariness in travel, and a necklace of peony beads could protect a young child from convulsions.

But it is the black magic—the forces of evil, both supernatural and human—that we chiefly associate with poisonous plants. Such herbs were used by witches to cast cruel spells and by ordinary people to damage their enemies. And yet, at the same time, all these baleful plants were important tools in the healing hands of physicians. For thousands of years they have brought life as well as death.

The rootstocks and leaves of Christmas rose contain two very toxic glucosides. All parts of the plant, when crushed, can cause a severe rash in some people. Called black hellebore because of the color of its roots, it was used 1,500 years before Christ by Greek physicians, who considered it a sure antidote to madness. In 1663, the herbalist William Turner wrote that it would cure those possessed of the Devil, and it was also used to treat deafness caused by witchcraft. It was always dug with mystic rites.

CHRISTMAS ROSE
Helleborus niger

THE MEDICINES

With its roots deep in this lore of sorcerers, the history of herbal medicine is a history also of magic, alchemy, and the occult. In fact, we can scarcely tell where medicine leaves off and magic begins, since most magic plants have some healing chemicals and most true medicines have been used in superstitious ways. Primitive people believed that disease came not from natural causes, but from evil powers exerted by demons or human enemies. So the use of herbs was part of a therapy that involved charms and rituals and was at first performed only by priests. In ancient Greece, people went to be healed by priests of the god Asclepius; in northern Europe, they turned to the Druids; and in North America the Indians consulted their medicine men. The very word "pharmacy" comes from an ancient Greek term for making magic.

Our real scientific knowledge of plants began when Greek scholars first compiled the herbal and medicinal information that had been accumulating in the Mediterranean region for thousands of years. By 300 B.C. they were describing the medicinal virtues of about five hundred plants. And more than half of those five hundred remained in use until the twentieth century.

Though the Romans were enthusiastic gardeners, they produced little new knowledge. But they did preserve botanical lore and spread it throughout their far-flung empire. And it was a Roman doctor of Greek origin, Dioscorides, who about A.D. 50 compiled a book called *De Materia Medica* that was the basis of herbal medicine for more than a thousand years.

Then, during the so-called Dark Ages in Europe, all this precious knowledge almost disappeared. It was saved only by monks who grew the plants in their physic gardens and used them to treat the sick, with the guidance of Dioscorides' herbal. They preserved all the ancient books and copied and recopied them. But nothing new was written until the Renaissance dawned, with its spirit of inquiry and its invention of printing. Then, with fresh curiosity, men began to examine their long-sacred medical traditions, and their writings ushered in the age of the great European herbals.

These herbals were mostly plant descriptions compiled for medical purposes, but they told a lot about gardening and also about magic and astrology. Every conceivable illness had its herbal cure. And there were also plants to be used for bites of dragons, for nightmares and melancholy, and for getting rid of "proud and superfluous flesh."

In the sixteenth and seventeenth centuries, most European doctors were influenced by the Doctrine of Signatures. They believed that "God maketh herbs for the use of man . . . and hath stamped upon them a distinct forme . . . whereby a man may read . . . the use of them." This meant that some

Digitalis has been used for centuries as a heart medicine, and it is still an important drug. European apothecaries prescribed it also for several other ailments. In the early nineteenth century, poor English-women sometimes drank it as a cheap means of intoxication. But foxglove was also a very special fairy flower, a hiding place for elves. It protected humans against fairy pranks and charms, and it brought back children stolen by elves.

FOXGLOVE
Digitalis purpurea

In Greek legend, poppies always crowned the twin gods of sleep and death. The Greeks believed that Demeter, in her grief over the loss of her daughter Persephone, created the poppy so she might obtain sleep. Its opium is still an important medicine, grown chiefly in the Far East, where the poppy plants yield especially large amounts of the drug. Seeds of poppies are not narcotic and have been used since prehistoric times in food and as a source of oil.

OPIUM POPPY
Papaver somniferum

HENBANE
Hyocyamus niger

These related plants have been in use for centuries. The ancients placed henbane on tombs and believed that it was worn around the heads of the dead in Hades. It stupifies animals, and at one time its seeds were mixed in the feed of horses and cows to make them docile. Introduced into the New World, it now grows wild in many places here. Belladonna is often called deadly nightshade. Its scientific name comes from one of the three Fates—Atropos, who cuts the thread of life. It has always been a valued drug, though a dangerous one. An herbalist called it "this naughtie and deadly plant."

This recipe also contained poison hemlock and henbane. Henbane, belladonna, and thorn apple all belong to the same family as tomato and potato, but all three are extremely poisonous. Their leaves, roots, and seeds contain the potent alkaloids atropine and hyoscyamine, which work on the central nervous system. From remote times, henbane—strange-looking and unattractive— was considered a plant of ill omen. But it was also used medicinally for its hypnotic and sedative properties, and necklaces of the root were put on children to prevent fits and to make teething easier. In modern medicine, hyoscyamine is an ingredient in the drug that produces "twilight sleep" in childbirth; and most wartime brainwashing of prisoners included hyoscyamine.

BELLADONNA
Atropa belladonna

THORN APPLE
Datura stramonium

Thorn apple for centuries has been connected with witchcraft and horror. Priests of Apollo used it to produce trances and prophetic ravings. The English brought the plant to North America, where it became a pest around their first colony at Jamestown and thus acquired the American name jimsonweed. Captain John Smith, governor of the colony, recorded the mad antics of some of his men who ate the seeds. The Incas of Peru used a South American species as an anesthetic. And a Colombian tribe gave it to wives and slaves before burying them alive with dead warriors.

51

Belladonna—"beautiful lady"—was so called because Italian woman used it to dilate the pupils of their eyes and thus make them seem dark and glamorous. It is still used by some eye specialists to dilate pupils, and until recently doctors prescribed it to relieve the spasms of asthma. The drug comes from the root, but every part of the plant is very poisonous. The dark-purple berries, with their inky juice, are intensely sweet—tempting and dangerous to children.

Thorn apple, or jimsonweed, is another ancient medicine, very similar to belladonna. All its parts, but especially the seeds, contain poisonous hyoscyamine, which can produce hallucinations and unconsciousness. Children have died after sucking the sweet nectar of its flowers. In ancient times, thieves knew that if it was swallowed in beer, it would cause madness for twenty-four hours, so they sometimes gave it to those they intended to rob. In Europe, a salve of thorn apple boiled in hog's grease was widely used for burns and inflammations, and John Parkinson recommends it as a drink for "one that is to have a legge or an arme cut off."

Almost to the present day, doctors have continued to use these and many other plant drugs, among them monkshood, lily of the valley, autumn crocus, and valerian. Valerian is rich in a volatile oil that, from Roman times onward, was considered a universal panacea. It is now valued for its sedative effect on the cerebrospinal system, and was widely used in wartime England to soothe shattered nerves during air raids.

Lily of the valley was also used in wartime, to treat soldiers

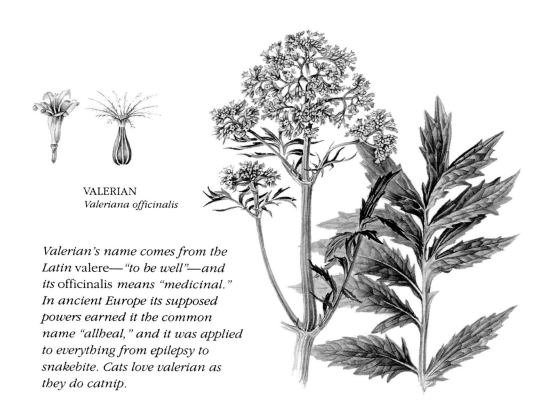

VALERIAN
Valeriana officinalis

Valerian's name comes from the Latin valere— *"to be well"—and its* officinalis *means "medicinal." In ancient Europe its supposed powers earned it the common name "allheal," and it was applied to everything from epilepsy to snakebite. Cats love valerian as they do catnip.*

injured by poison gas. Its dried flowers, and to a lesser extent its roots and leaves, have an action on the heart similar to that of digitalis. The ancient herbalists prescribed it for palsy and other nervous afflictions, and for eye inflammations.

Autumn crocus has long been a treatment for gout, prized by Egyptian, Greek, and Arab doctors, and later by European apothecaries. When its colchicine was finally analyzed at the end of the eighteenth century, it became an official drug, the standard treatment for gout. Today it is most widely used to produce new varieties of garden flowers by altering their chromosome numbers. And it has recently been studied as a possible treatment for multiple sclerosis.

LILY OF THE VALLEY
Convallaria majalis

Lily of the valley is also called May lily or Our Lady's tears. It was brought to North America from Europe and is mostly a garden plant here, but it often escapes and grows wild. Since medieval times, it has been valued as a medicine and was held in such great repute that liquid distilled from its blossoms was kept only in vessels of gold or silver. Lily of the valley extract is so toxic that four drops injected into a dog will kill it in ten minutes.

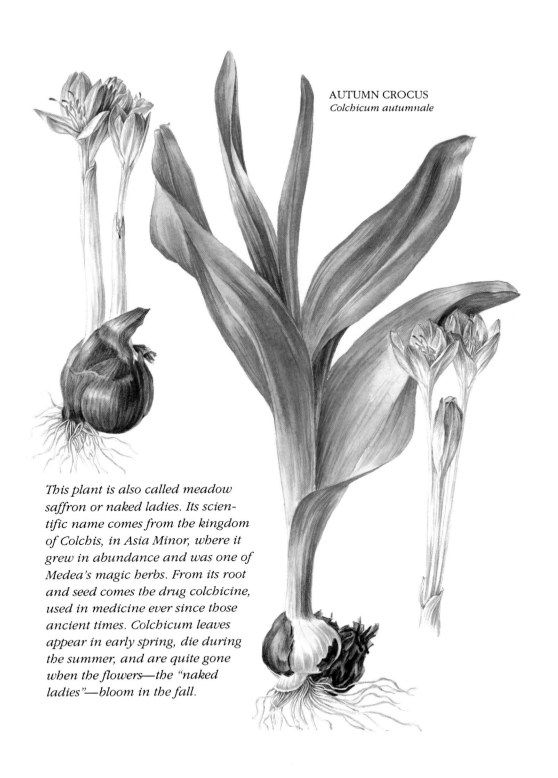

AUTUMN CROCUS
Colchicum autumnale

This plant is also called meadow saffron or naked ladies. Its scientific name comes from the kingdom of Colchis, in Asia Minor, where it grew in abundance and was one of Medea's magic herbs. From its root and seed comes the drug colchicine, used in medicine ever since those ancient times. Colchicum leaves appear in early spring, die during the summer, and are quite gone when the flowers—the "naked ladies"—bloom in the fall.

GOLDENSEAL
Hydrastis canadensis

All these plants came to the New World after their long medical history in Europe and Asia. As late as 1955, they were all to be found in the United States Pharmacopoeia, the official list of drugs in use. But the Americas also contributed their own healing plants, most of them known and used by the Indians. Over fifty of these American natives were in the Pharmacopoeia well into the twentieth century, and a few still are there.

The first North American colonists practiced folk medicine just as their European ancestors did. Farm wives learned from Indian wives and prepared the remedies for their own families. As doctors became more numerous, they too drew from the Indians, adding to their ancient remedies the new American herbs that they collected and prepared themselves. Through most of the nineteenth century, every doctor was also a botanist and pharmacist.

These doctors used mayapple as a purgative, Carolina jessamine as a sedative and to relieve spasms, pinkroot to kill intestinal worms. Goldenseal soothed inflammations of the digestive tract, and dogbane was a heart tonic. The rhizome and roots of false hellebore were used for brain ailments. Indian tobacco was smoked and chewed by the Indians, and recently it has become an important aid to people giving up smoking. The poisonous rhizome of bloodroot was used chiefly to induce vomiting, but was also applied in the treatment of many other ailments. All these plants, which still

DOGBANE
Apocynum androsaemifolium

American Indians used the root of goldenseal as a medicine and its yellow juice as a dye. Until recently, it was an official drug in the Pharmacopoeia. Two common species of dogbane are very much alike in appearance and action:

A. androsaemifolium *is a heart tonic much like digitalis, but it has extremely irritating side effects. A.* cannabinum, *also a heart medicine, is sometimes called Indian hemp because its fiber has been used to make twine.*

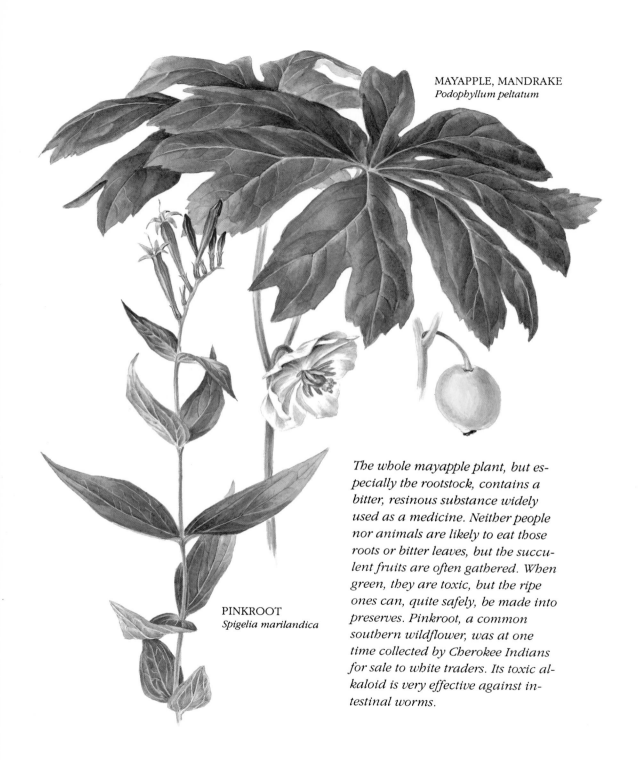

MAYAPPLE, MANDRAKE
Podophyllum peltatum

PINKROOT
Spigelia marilandica

The whole mayapple plant, but especially the rootstock, contains a bitter, resinous substance widely used as a medicine. Neither people nor animals are likely to eat those roots or bitter leaves, but the succulent fruits are often gathered. When green, they are toxic, but the ripe ones can, quite safely, be made into preserves. Pinkroot, a common southern wildflower, was at one time collected by Cherokee Indians for sale to white traders. Its toxic alkaloid is very effective against intestinal worms.

This species of Veratrum, *a common American plant, is not likely to tempt either man or animal because of its sharp, burning taste. But it grows among other wild plants that are edible, and its young shoots can easily be gathered accidentally. It is intensely narcotic, and its roots have been used in medicine to lower blood pressure. Jessamine roots, leaves, and flowers are all poisonous, containing an alkaloid similar to strychnine. Its roots have been an official drug.*

FALSE HELLEBORE
Veratrum viride

CAROLINA JESSAMINE
Gelsemium sempervirens

grow wild in many parts of the United States, are easily found. But now country people—wisely—no longer treat themselves. The plants are all poisonous, and overdoses can well be fatal.

Though the basic chemicals of these old herbal drugs are still used by doctors, they are today nearly all synthesized. But this does not mean that there is no longer any interest in living medicinal plants. Since World War II there has been a tremendous flurry of activity in the search for new healing herbs all over the world. Drug companies, alarmed by the vanishing forests and the disappearing witch doctors, have sent small armies of botanists to the most remote lands. They are looking into the magic and medicine of primitive tribes, and gathering folklore, information, and plant specimens. And they have made a number of dramatic discoveries. In 1952, rauwolfia, used in the folk medicine of India, was found to produce a drug that became one of the first important tranquilizers. Cortisone is produced from a Central American yam. Madagascar periwinkle has proved very effective against several forms of cancer. The South American arrow poison curare is the source of a substance that relaxes muscles and is now used in almost all anesthesia.

No one knows how many plants with similar powers still hide in the distant rich forests of South America, Asia, and Africa, locked away among vast numbers of unknown species. And if the ruthless destruction of the world's precious forests is not halted soon, no one will ever know what we have lost there.

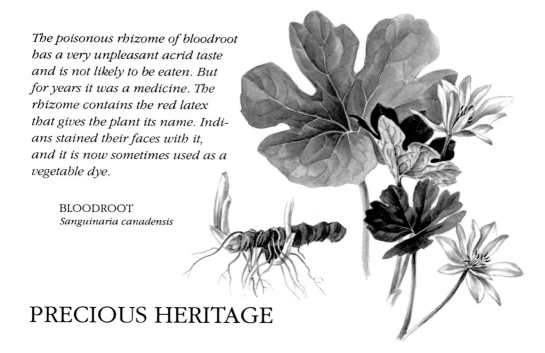

The poisonous rhizome of bloodroot has a very unpleasant acrid taste and is not likely to be eaten. But for years it was a medicine. The rhizome contains the red latex that gives the plant its name. Indians stained their faces with it, and it is now sometimes used as a vegetable dye.

BLOODROOT
Sanguinaria canadensis

PRECIOUS HERITAGE

Mankind is still dependent on the green world. Even though we are now able to manufacture most of the products our daily lives demand, plants will continue to provide our food and many of the raw materials for our factories.

Our medicines and insecticides and rat baits no longer come entirely from the poisonous plants that still grow all around us. But we should know about those plants. They can be dangerous, even though over the centuries they have always done almost as much healing as harming. But even if they do no healing at all, they are precious. Nearly all are beautiful and interesting, and they are never sinister if we approach them with knowledge and respect.

61

Index of Plants

Numbers in **bold** indicate illustrations

Subject Index

Numbers in **bold** indicate illustrations